Books For Kids:

Joke Book for Kids
(Children's Book)

(Knock Knock, Animal Jokes, Tongue Twisters, Riddles)

Jessica Child

For my lovely students

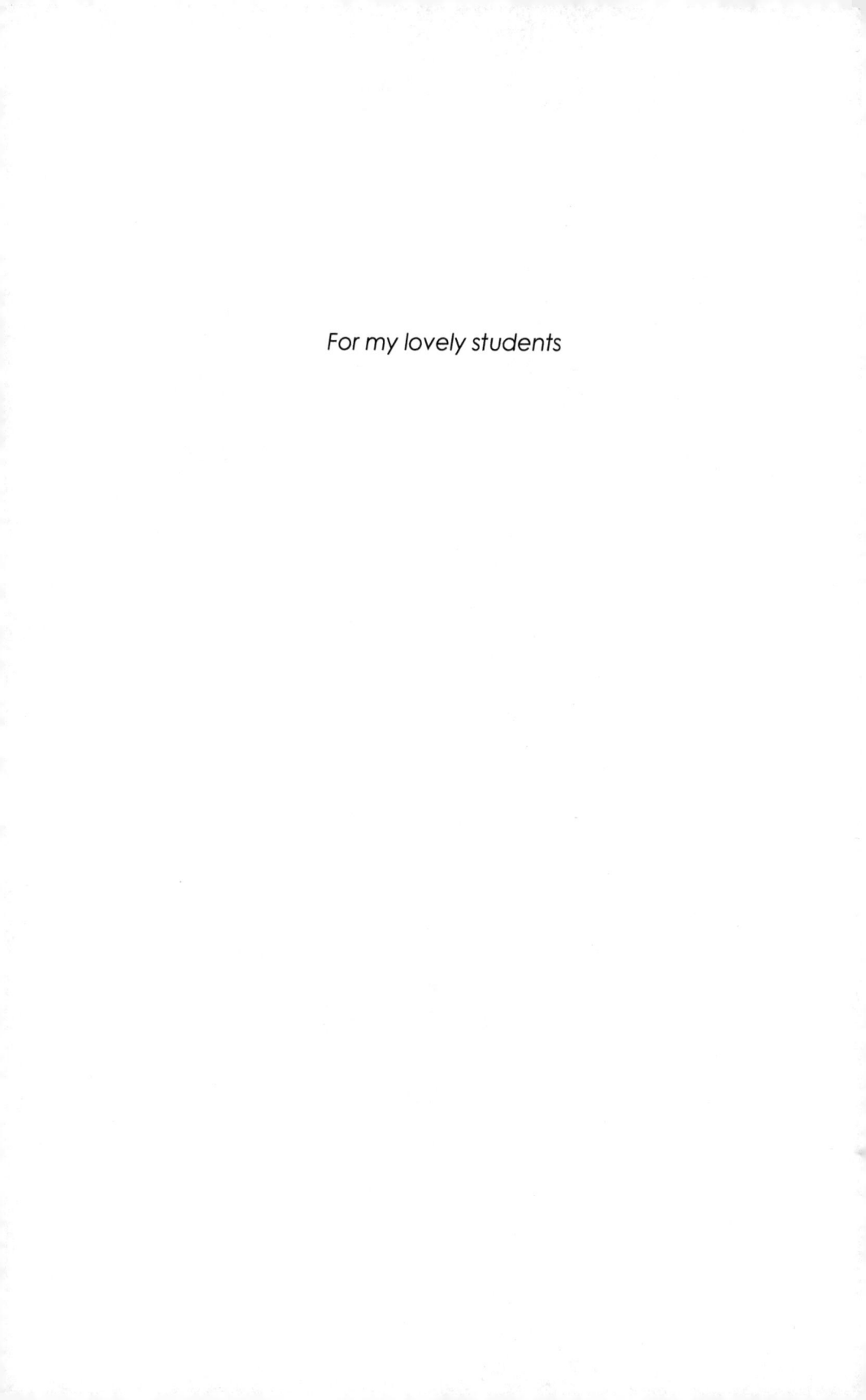

Copyright © 2014 Jessica Child
All rights reserved.

CONTENTS

Animal Jokes

Knock Knock Jokes

Tongue Twisters

Funny Puns

Funny Riddles

Animal Jokes

Q: Why did the cat go to Minnesota?
A: To get a mini soda!

Q: Where do orcas hear music?
A: Orca-stras!

Q: Why did the cow cross the road?
A: To get to the udder side.

Q: What do you call a fish without an eye?
A: Fsh!

Q: What do you do if your dog chews a dictionary?
A: Take the words out of his mouth!

Q: What do you call a cold dog sitting on a bunny?
A: A chili dog on a bun.

Q: Why do fish live in salt water?
A: Because pepper makes them sneeze!

Q: Where do mice park their boats?
A: At the hickory dickory dock.

Q: Where did the sheep go on vacation?
A: The baaaahamas

Q: What do you call a thieving alligator?
A: A crookodile

Q: What goes tick-tock, bow-wow, tick-tock, bow-wow?
A: A watch dog.

Q: What do you call a cow that eats your grass?
A: A lawn moo-er.

Q: What do you call a girl with a frog on her head?
A: Lilly.

Q: How does a dog stop a video?
A: He presses the paws button.

Q: Why do cows go to New York?
A: To see the moosicals!

Q: What do you call lending money to a bison?
A: A buff-a-loan

Q: What is the snake's favorite subject?
A: Hiss-story

Q: What is black ,white and red all over?
A: A sunburnt penguin!

Q: Why does a dog wag its tail?
A: Because there's no one else to wag it for him.

Q: What is a cat's favorite movie?
A: The sound of Mew-sic!

Q: How do you make a goldfish old?
A: Take away the g!

Q: Why did the lamb cross the road?
A: To get to the baaaaarber shop!

Q: How does a mouse feel after it takes a shower?
A: Squeaky clean!

Q: What has four legs and goes "Oom, Oom"?
A: A cow walking backwards!

Q: Where do you put barking dogs?
A: In a barking lot.

Q: What do you call a pig that's been arrested for dangerous driving?
A: A road hog.

Q: What is a cheetahs favorite food?
A: Fast food!

A team of little animals and a team of big animals decided to play football. During the first half of the game, the big animals were winning. But during the second half,a centipede scored so many touchdowns that the little animals won the game. When the game was over, the chipmunk asked the centipede, "Where were you during the first half?" He replied "Putting on my shoes!".

Q: What does a cat say when somebody steps on its tail?
A: Me-ow!

Q: What do you call a baby bear with no teeth?
A: A gummy bear!

Q: Why did the dog cross the road twice?
A: He was trying to fetch a boomerang!

Q: What is as big as an elephant but weighs nothing?
A: Its shadow!

Q: What do you call a pig who knows karate?
A: Porkchop!

Q: Where does an elephant pack his luggage?
A: In his trunk!

Q: There were 10 cats in a boat and one jumped out. How many were left?
A: None, because they were copycats!

Q: Which day do fish hate?
A: Fryday!

Q: What do you call a cow in a tornado?
A: A milkshake!

Q: What did the peanut say to the elephant?
A: Nothing, peanuts don't talk.

Q: What do you call a deer with no eyes?
A: No I deer!

Q: Why was the cat afraid of a tree?
A: Because of the bark!

Q: How are elephants and trees alike?
A: They both have trunks!

Q: What do you call an exploding monkey?
A: A baboom!

Q: What do you call an elephant in a phone booth?
A: Stuck!

Q: What do you call a sleeping bull?
A: A bulldozer!

Q. How do you stop a dog barking in the back seat of a car?
A. Put him in the front seat.

Q: What is the difference between a car and a bull?
A: A car only has one horn.

Q: What did the carrot say to the rabbit?
A: Do you want to grab a bite?

Q: What time is it when an elephant sits on your bed?
A: Time to get a new bed!

Q: Where does a ten ton elephant sit?
A: Anywhere it wants to!

Q: What was the first animal in space?
A: The cow that jumped over the moon!

Q: What do you get when you plant a frog?
A: A cr-oak tree.

Q: What is the quietest kind of a dog?
A: A hush puppy.

Q: How is a dog like a telephone?
A: It has a collar I.D.

Q: Why do cows wear bells?
A: Because their horns don't work.

There were two cows in a field. The first cow said "moo" and the second cow said "baaaa." The first cow asked the second cow, "why did you say baaaa?" The second cow said, "I'm learning a foreign language."

Q: How do you stop an elephant from charging?
A: Take away his credit card!

Q: Why do you bring fish to a party?
A: Because it goes good with chips.

Q: What would happen if pigs could fly?
A: The price of bacon would go up.

Q: How do you get a dog to stop digging in the garden?
A: Take away his shovel!

Q: What did the frog say when he heard "time flies when you are having fun?"
A: Time is fun when you're having flies!

Q: What did the grape say when the elephant stepped on it?
A: It gave a little wine!

Q: Why would an elephant paint its toenails different colors?
A: To hide in a bag of M&M's.

Q: How do you catch a squirrel?
A: Climb up a tree and act like a nut!

Q: Where do fish keep their money?
A: In a river bank!

A duck, a skunk and a deer went out for dinner at a restaurant one night. When it came time to pay, the skunk didn't have a scent, the deer didn't have a buck so they put the meal on the duck's bill.

Q: What did one cow say to the other?
A: Mooooooove over!

Q: What kind of cat should you never play games with?
A: A cheetah!

Q: Why did the turtle cross the road?
A: To get to the shell station.

Q: What is black and white and red all over?
A: A skunk with a rash.

Q: What time is it when 5 dogs chase 1 cat?
A: Five after one.

Q: What do whales eat?
A: Fish and ships.

Q: What part of a fish weighs the most?
A: The scales.

Q: What do you call a dinosaur in a car accident?
A: A tyrannosauraus wreck!

Q: What did the banana do when the monkey chased it?
A: The banana split!

Q: What's the difference between a fish and a piano?
A: You can't tuna fish.

Q: What do you call a gorilla wearing earmuffs?
A: Anything you like, he can't hear you.

Q: Why are giraffes so slow to apologize?
A: It takes them a long time to swallow their pride.

Q: How did Noah see the animals in the Ark at night?
A: With flood lighting.

Q: What is the easiest way to count a herd of cattle?
A: With a cowculator.

Q: What did the farmer call the cow that would not give

him any milk?
A: An udder failure.

Q: Why did the cow cross the road?
A: Because the chicken was on vacation.

Q: What do you get from a bad-tempered shark?
A: As far away as possible.

Q: What did the sardine call the submarine?
A: A can of people.

Q: What fish only swims at night?
A: A starfish.

Q: Why did the elephant leave the circus?
A: He was tired of working for peanuts.

There were two cows in a paddock. One of the cows says, "moo" and the other one says, "That's what I was going to say."

Customer: "Do you have alligator shoes?"
Clerk: "Yes, sir. What size does your alligator wear?"

Q: What do you get when you cross a roll of wool and a kangaroo?
A: A woolen jumper!

Q: What did the Cinderella fish wear to the ball?
A: Glass flippers.

Q: Why was the mouse afraid of the water?
A: Catfish

Q: What happened when the lion ate the comedian?
A: He felt funny.

Q: How many skunks does it take to make a big stink?
A: A phew.

Q: Why did the policeman give the sheep a ticket?
A: He was a baaaaaaaaad driver.

Q: How do you keep a skunk from smelling?
A: Plug its nose.

Q: What has four legs, a trunk, and sunglasses?
A: A mouse on vacation.

Q: What do you call a 400-pound gorilla?
A: Sir.

Q: What's black and white and red all over?
A: A blushing zebra.

Q: What is a cow's favorite place?
A: The mooseum.

Q: What do fish take to stay healthy?
A: Vitamin sea.

Q: What do you call a mommy cow that just had a calf?
A: Decalfinated!

Q: What do you call a mad elephant?
A: An earthquake.

Q: What is a shark's favorite sandwich?
A: Peanut butter and jellyfish.

Q: Where are sharks from?
A: Finland.

Q: What is King Arthur's favorite fish?
A: A swordfish

Q: Why did the policeman give the sheep a ticket?
A: He made an illegal ewe turn.

Q: What does an octopus wear when it gets cold?
A: A coat of arms.

Q: What kind of dog always runs a fever?
A: A hot dog!

Q: What did the momma buffalo say to her son before he went to school?
A: Bison!

Q: What has 4 wheels, gives milk, and eats grass.
A: A cow on a skateboard.

Q: Why don't bears wear shoes?
A: What's the use, they'd still have bear feet!

Q: What do you call a dog that likes bubble baths?
A: A shampoodle!

Q: What does a calf become after it's 1 year old?
A: 2 years old.

Cow: "Mooooove over!"
Sheep: "Naaaaaaa."

Q: How do you know an elephant has been in your refrigerator?
A: There are footprints in the butter.

Q: Why does a giraffe have such a long neck?
A: Because his feet stink!

Q: What's a dog's favorite food for breakfast?
A: Pooched eggs.

Q: What do you give a pig with a rash?
A: Oinkment.

Q: What do you do if your cat swallows your pencil?
A: Use a pen.

Q: What's black and white, black and white, black and white and green?
A: Three skunks fighting over a pickle!

First dog: My master calls me Furball. How about you?
Second Dog: My master calls me Sitboy!

Q: What kind of mouse does not eat, drink, or even walk?
A: A computer mouse.

Q: What do you call a dog with a Rolex?
A: A watch dog.

Q: What pine has the longest needles?
A: A porcupine.

Q: What's worse than a centipede with athlete's foot?
A: A porcupine with split ends!

Q: Why did the dinosaur cross the road?
A: The chicken wasn't around yet.

Q: What kind of cars do cats drive?
A: Catillacs!

Q: What do you call a deer that costs a dollar?
A: A buck.

Q: What's a frog's favorite drink?
A: Croak-a-cola.

Q: What's an alligator's favorite drink?
A: Gator-Ade.

Q: What do you call snake with no clothes on?
A: Snaked.

Q: What did the dog say to the flea?
A: Stop bugging me!

Q: Where do cows go on Saturday night?
A: To the moooooovies.

Q: What do you call a dinosaur that never gives up?
A: A try and try and try-ceratops!

Q: What do you call a dinosaur at the rodeo?
A: A Broncosaurus or a Tyrannosaurus Tex.

Q: What has ears like a cat and a tail like a cat, but is not a cat?
A: A kitten.

Q: Who makes dinosaur clothes?
A: A dino-sewer.

Q: What did the snail say when he got on the turtle's shell?
A: Weeeeeeeeeeeeeeeeeeeeeeeeee!

Q: Where do sheep get their hair cut?
A: At the baa-baa shop.

Q: Why can't hippos ride bicycles?
A: Bike helmets don't fit hippos!

Q: What's a puppy's favorite kind of pizza?
A: Pupperoni.

Q: What's black and white and red all over?
A: A sunburnt zebra.

Q: What happened when 500 hares got loose on Main Street?
A: The police had to comb the area.

Q: What do camels use to hide themselves?
A: Camelflauge!

Q: What do you call a messy hippo?
A: A hippopota-mess!

Q: What do you call a cow that twitches?
A: Beef jerky

Q: What did the porcupine say to the cactus?
A: Is that you mommy?

Q: What is a lion's favorite state?
A: Maine

Q: Where do horses live?
A: In the neigh-borhood.

Q: Why are elephants wrinkled?
A: Because they don't fit on a ironing board!

Q: What is a cat's favorite breakfast?
A: Mice krispies

Q: What is a frog's favorite year?
A: Leap Year

Q: What kind of dog has a bark but no bite?
A: A Dogwood!

Q: What is a pirate's favorite's fish?
A: A swordfish!

Q: What is a horse's favorite sport?
A: Stable tennis!

Q: Why do pandas like old movies?
A: Because they are black and white.

Q: How many sheep do you need to make a sweater?
A: I don't know. I didn't think sheep could knit!

Q: What do you call a bruise on a T-Rex?
A: A dino-sore!

Q: What game do elephants play when riding in the back of a car?
A: Squash!

Knock Knock Jokes

Knock, knock.

Who's there?

Canoe.

Canoe who?

Canoe help me with my homework?

Knock, knock

Who's there?

Merry.

Merry who?

Merry Christmas!

Knock, knock.

Who's there?

Orange.

Orange who?

Orange you going to let me in?

Knock, knock.

Who's there?

Anee.

Anee, who?

Anee one you like!

Knock, knock

Who's there?

Iva.

Iva who?

I've a sore hand from knocking!

Knock, knock.

Who's there?

Dozen.

Dozen who?

Dozen anybody want to let me in?

Knock, knock.

Who's there?

Needle.

Needle who?

Needle little money for the movies.

Knock, knock.

Who's there?

Henrietta.

Henrietta who?

Henrietta worm that was in his apple.

Knock, knock.

Who's there?

Avenue.

Avenue who?

Avenue knocked on this door before?

Knock, knock.

Who's there?

Harry.

Harry who?

Harry up, it's cold out here!

Knock, knock.

Who's there?

A herd.

A herd who?

A herd you were home, so I came over!

Knock, knock.

Who's there?

Adore.

Adore who?

Adore is between us. Open up!

Knock, knock.

Who's there?

Otto.

Otto who?

Otto know. I've got amnesia.

Knock, knock.

Who's there?

King Tut.

King Tut who?

King Tut-key fried chicken!

Knock, knock.

Who's there?

Lettuce.

Lettuce who?

Lettuce in it's cold out here.

Knock, knock.

Who's there?

Noah.

Noah who?

Noah good place we can get something to eat?

Knock, knock.

Who's there?

Robin.

Robin who?

Robin the piggy bank again.

Knock, knock.

Who's there?

Dwayne.

Dwayne who?

Dwayne the bathtub, It's overflowing!

Knock, knock.

Who's There?

Imma.

Imma Who?

Imma gettin' old open the door!

Knock, knock.

Who's there?

Boo.

Boo who?

Gosh, don't cry it's just a knock knock joke.

Knock, knock.

Who's There?

Impatient cow.

Impatient cow wh-?

Mooooo!

Knock, knock

Who's there?

A little old lady.

A little old lady who?

I didn't know you could yodel.

Knock, knock

Who's there?

Sadie.

Sadie who?

Sadie magic word and watch me disappear!

Knock, knock,

Who's there?

Olive.

Olive who?

Olive you!

Knock, knock.

Who's there?

Justin.

Justin who?

Justin time for dinner.

Knock, knock.

Who's there?

Kirtch.

Kirtch who?

God bless you!

Knock, knock.

Who's there?

Luke.

Luke who?

Luke through the the peep hole and find out.

Knock, knock.

Who's there?

Ivor.

Ivor who?

Ivor you let me in or I`ll climb through the window.

Knock Knock!

Who's there?

Doughnut!

Doughnut who?

Doughnut ask, it's a secret.

Knock Knock!

Who's there?

Justin!

Justin who?

Justin time for lunch.

Knock Knock!

Who's there?

Broccoli.

Broccoli who?

Broccoli doesn't have a last name, silly.

Knock Knock!

Who's there?

Figs.

Figs who?

Figs the doorbell, it's broken!

Knock Knock!

Who's there?

Cash.

Cash who?

I knew you were a nut!

Knock Knock!

Who's there?

Olive.

Olive who?

Olive right next to you.

Knock Knock!

Who's there?

Orange.

Orange who?

Orange you glad I'm here?

Knock Knock!

Who's there?

Dishe.s

Dishes who?

Dishes me, who are you?

Knock Knock!

Who's there?

Who.

Who who?

Are you an owl?

Knock Knock!

Who's there?

Cowsgo.

Cowsgo who?

No they don't, cowsgo moo.

Knock Knock!

Who's there?

Interrupting cow.

Interrupt...

Moo!

Knock Knock!

Who's there?

Kook!

Kook who?

Don't call me cuckoo!

Knock Knock!

Who's there?

Boo!

Boo who?

Don't cry, it's just me.

Knock Knock!

Who's there?

Abby!

Abby who?

Abby birthday to you.

Knock Knock!

Who's there?

Tarzan!

Tarzan who?

Tarzan stripes forever.

Knock Knock!

Who's there?

Doris!

Doris who?

Doris locked, that's why I knocked.

Knock Knock!

Who's there?

Avenue!

Avenue who?

Avenue heard this joke before.

Knock Knock!

Who's there?

Canoe!

Canoe who?

Canoe come over and play.

Knock knock!

Who's there?

Little old lady?

Little old lady who?

Wow! I didn't know you could yodel!

Knock knock!

Who's there?

Water?

Water who?

Water way to answer the door!

Knock knock!

Who's there?

Leaf?

Leaf who?

Leaf me alone!

Knock knock!

Who's there?

Cargo!

Cargo who?

Car go "Beep beep"!

Knock knock!

Who's there?

Dewey.

Dewey who?

Dewey have to keep telling silly jokes.

Knock Knock

Who's there?

Irish!

Irish who?

Irish you a happy St. Patrick's Day.

Knock, knock

Who's there?

You

You who?

Isn't that a drink?!

Knock, knock

Who's there?

Goliath

Goliath who?

Goliath down you're lookin' tired.

Knock, knock

Who's there?

Boo

Boo who?

Didn't mean to scare you!

Knock, knock

Who's there?

Atch

Atch who?

Oh, I'm sorry. I didn't know you had a cold.

Knock, knock

Who's there?

Peas

Peas who?

Peas let me in now!

Knock, knock

Who's there?

Tickle

Tickle who?

Tickle you.

Knock, knock

Who's there?

Aliens

Aliens who?

Just how many aliens do you know?

Knock, knock

Who's there?

Bo

Bo who?

That's bogus!

Knock, knock

Who's there?

Dwain

Dwain who?

Dwain the bathtub, I'm drowning.

Knock, knock

Who's there?

Let us

Let us who?

Let us in, it's raining!

Knock, knock

Who's there?

Butch

Butch who?

Butch you little arms around me!

Knock, knock

Who's there?

Some bunny

Some bunny who?

Some bunny has been eating my carrots!

Knock, knock

Who's there?

Come in...

Knock, knock

Who's there?

Cash

Cash who?

No thanks, I prefer peanuts!

Knock, knock

Who's there?

Ya

Ya who?

What are you so excited about?

Knock, knock

Who's there?

Armageddon

Armageddon who?

Armageddon out of here if you don't let me in!

Knock, knock

Who's there?

Ivan

Ivan who?

Ivan. You lose!

Knock, knock

Who's there?

Repeat

Repeat who?

Who, who, who...

Knock, knock

Who's there?

Brittney Spears.

Brittney Spears who?

Knock, knock

Who's there?

Oops! I did it again!

Knock, knock

Who's there?

Boo

Boo who?

Why are you crying?

Knock, knock

Who's there?

Hada

Hada who?

Had a great time, how about you?

Knock, knock

Who's there?

Cargo

Cargo who?

Cargo beep, beep!

Knock, knock

Who's there?

Twit

Twit who?

Did anyone else hear an owl?

Knock, knock

Who's there?

Dwayne

Dwayne who?

Dwayne the bathtub, I'm Dwowning!

Knock, knock

Who's there?

G.I.

G.I. who?

G.I. don't know?

Knock, knock

Who's there?

Lettuce

Lettuce who?

Lettuce in!

Knock, knock

Who's there?

Boo

Boo who?

Don't cry, it's only a joke.

Knock, knock

Who's there?

Echo

Echo who?

Echo who? Echo who?

Knock, knock

Who's there?

Scold

Scold who?

Scold outside!

Knock, knock

Who's there?

Shocking

Shocking who?

Shocking you!

Knock, knock

Who's there?

Zee

Zee who?

Can't you zee I'm knocking?!

Knock, knock

Who's there?

You haven't even opened the door yet!

Knock, knock

Who's there?

Zaire

Zaire who?

Zaire is polluted!

Knock, knock

Who's there?

You

You who?

I didn't know you were so happy to meet me!

Knock, knock

Who's there?

Lena

Lena who?

Lena little closer and I'll tell you!

Knock, knock

Who's there?

Monkey

Monkey who?

Monkey see. Monkey do.

Knock, knock

Who's there?

Double

Double who?

W!

Knock, knock

Who's there?

Justin

Justin who?

Just in time for school!

Knock, knock

Who's there?

Icy

Icy who?

Icy you!

Knock knock

Who's there?

Mikey!

Mikey who?

Mikey doesn't fit in the keyhole!

Knock knock

Who's there?

Howard!

Howard who?

Howard I know?

Knock knock

Who's there?

Beets!

Beets who?

Beets me!

Knock knock

Who's there?

Ice cream!

Ice cream who?

Ice cream if you don't let me in!

Knock knock

Who's there?

Cows!

Cows who?

Cows go 'moo' not who!

Knock knock

Who's there?

A titch!

A titch who?

Bless you!

Knock knock

Who's there?

Tank!

Tank who?

You're welcome!

Knock knock

Who's there?

Luke!

Luke who?

Luke through the keyhole and you can see!

Knock knock

Who's there?

Frank!

Frank who?

Frank you for being my friend!

Knock knock

Who's there?

Wooden shoe!

Wooden shoe who?

Wooden shoe like to hear another joke?

Knock, knock

Who's There?

Barbie

Barbie Who?

Barbie Q Chicken!

Knock, knock

Who's there?

Figs

Figs who?

Figs the doorbell, it's broken!

Tongue Twisters

Eleven owls licked eleven little liquorice lollipops.

Greek grapes, Greek grapes, Greek grapes...

I scream you scream we all scream for ice cream...

She sells sea shells by the sea shore.

Kitty caught the kitten in the kitchen.

Zebras zig and zebras zag.

If two witches were watching two watches, which witch would watch which watch?

The big bug bit the little beetle, but the little beetle bit the big bug back."

Red lorry, yellow lorry.

If you want to buy, buy, if you don't want to buy, bye bye!

Fuzzy wuzzy was a bear. Fuzzy wuzzy had no hair. Fuzzy wuzzy wasn't very fuzzy, was he?

The blue bluebird blinks.

A tricky frisky snake with sixty super scaly stripes.

I can think of six thin things, but I can think of six thick things too.

Toy phone, Toy phone, Toy phone...

Give papa a cup of proper coffee in a copper coffee cup.

Three free throws.

Not these things here, but those things there.

How much wood would a woodchuck chuck if a woodchuck could chuck wood?

A big black bug bit a big black dog on his big black nose.

Red leather yellow leather.

Quick kiss, quick kiss, quick kiss.

Friendly fleas and fireflies.

Fresh fried fish, fish fresh fried, fried fish fresh, fish fried fresh.

Mix a box of mixed biscuits with a boxed biscuit mixer.

A proper copper coffee pot.

I saw Esau sitting on a seesaw. Esau, he saw me.

Toy boat. Toy boat. Toy boat.

Lovely lemon liniment.

Six thick thistle sticks. Six thick thistles stick.

Good blood, bad blood.

Three free throws.The instinct of an extinct insect stinks.

Comical economists. Comical economists.

Which wristwatches are Swiss wristwatches?

Peter Piper picked a peck of pickled peppers.

A peck of pickled peppers Peter Piper picked.

If Peter Piper picked a peck of pickled peppers,

Where's the peck of pickled peppers Peter Piper picked?

World Wide Web

How many cookies could a good cook cook if a good cook could cook cookies? A good cook could cook as much cookies as a good cook who could cook cookies.

Black background, brown background.

Why do you cry, Willy?

Why do you cry?

Why, Willy?

Why, Willy?

Why, Willy? Why?

Six slimy snails sailed silently.

I thought, I thought of thinking of thanking you.

I wish to wash my Irish wristwatch.

Little Mike left his bike like Tike at Spike's.

Two tiny tigers take two taxis to town.

Tommy Tucker tried to tie Tammy's Turtles tie.

Double bubble gum, bubbles double.

She said she should sit.

She sees cheese.

Silly sheep weep and sleep.

Real weird rear wheels

Knife and a fork bottle and a cork

that is the way you spell New York.

Chicken in the car and the car can go,

that is the way you spell Chicago.

How much ground could a groundhog grind if a groundhog could grind ground?

How may saws could a see-saw saw if a see-saw could saw saws?

How much dew does a dewdrop drop

If dewdrops do drop dew?

They do drop, they do

As do dewdrops drop

If dewdrops do drop dew.

Come, come,

Stay calm, stay calm,

No need for alarm,

It only hums,

It doesn't harm.

Betty Botter bought some butter but, said she, the butter's bitter.

If I put it in my batter, it will make my batter bitter.

But a bit of better butter will make my bitter batter better.

So she bought some better butter, better than the bitter butter,

put it in her bitter batter, made her bitter batter better.

So 't was better Betty Botter bought some better butter.

I saw a saw that could out saw any other saw I ever saw.

A skunk sat on a stump and thunk the stump stunk,
but the stump thunk the skunk stunk.

Funny Puns

Puns are a form of word play which take advantage of words, or similar sounding words, with multiple meanings, often to create a humorous situation or joke

Let's talk about rights and lefts. You're right, so I left.

Time flies like an arrow. Fruit flies like a banana.

When a clock is hungry it goes back four seconds.

A boiled egg every morning is hard to beat.

Two fish are in a tank. One says to the other, "Err...so how do you drive this thing?"

I went to buy some camouflage trousers yesterday but couldn't find any.

I've been to the dentist many times so I know the drill.

Being struck by lightning is a shocking experience!

Without geometry, life is pointless.

A chicken crossing the road is truly poultry in motion.

I went to a seafood disco last week....and pulled a mussel.

She had a photographic memory but never developed it.

Two antennas met on a roof, fell in love and got married. The ceremony wasn't much, but the reception was brilliant!

Funny Riddles

Check out our funny riddles for kids and enjoy some great humor with a brain bending twist.

What has a face and two hands but no arms or legs? A clock

What five-letter word becomes shorter when you add two letters to it? Short

What word begins and ends with an 'e' but only has one letter? Envelope

What has a neck but no head? A bottle

What type of cheese is made backwards? Edam

What gets wetter as it dries? A towel

Why did the boy bury his flashlight? Because the batteries died.

Which letter of the alphabet has the most water? The C

What starts with a 'P', ends with an 'E' and has thousands of letters? The Post Office!

What has to be broken before you can use it? An egg

Why can't a man living in New York be buried in Chicago? Because he's still living!

What begins with T, ends with T and has T in it? A teapot

How many letters are there in the English alphabet? There are 18: 3 in 'the', 7 in 'English' and 8 in 'alphabet'.

Which month has 28 days? All of them of course!